Contents

Foreword

Theory has its place but, in a world that is changing at lightning speed, businesses learn best from those who have been there and done it – a few times. This brings me nicely to Wayne Wright.

He is a man with his sleeves constantly rolled up who has the generosity to share his experience, knowledge and sharp analytical mind with those in need of some inspiration.

This book has been a long time in coming but, believe me, it has been well worth waiting for. The gems just keep jumping off each page.

This is a practical and pragmatic guide, borne out of Wayne's close proximity to both thinking and action. There is no ego or showing off, just the will and desire to share what he has picked up over the years to benefit others. No business task has ever been too small for him, and no corporate challenge has ever been too big. From start-ups to multinationals, he has something to say to everyone.

I love his continuous gentle nudges to break away from the pull of the past and embrace new behaviours and attitudes. It's a real gift to get many people to realise that they have been solving the wrong problem really well. I laughed out loud when I realised I'd just been shown a far better way to approach the same issue he describes.

It's a fascinating, easy read that leaves you wanting to know more, and he answers every question that pops up in your mind almost straight way. The Ten Commandments of Business Growth is a charming and well-considered guide to growing any business.

When you've finished reading it, do someone you like a favour by giving them a copy.

René Carayol MBE

Acknowledgements

This book has been ten years in the making. Finding the time to finish off an idea that came through a dream has been a big 'bucket-list' item in my life.

I would like to acknowledge the loves of my life – my wife, Joanne, and my delightful young adults, André and his wife Stephanie, Micah and his wife Laura, and Anne-Marie. Thank you for your support and encouraging me to get this done.

To our many clients who have benefited from our input in growing their businesses, thank you for trusting us and well done for persevering and growing during challenging times.

I do believe that each person can make a difference in this life. My faith in God has helped me to utilise a gift of business wisdom that can help companies to grow. It has been a roller-coaster of a ride, but it's been great. As a Christian, I am humbled and grateful for being the custodian of such an incredible gift.

Preface

Why ten commandments? Why not eleven or twelve or even twenty commandments?

I'm sure that everyone will make a case for more commandments, but I wanted to focus on the top ten. The 'top ten' always has a ring about it; it signifies absolutes, numerical completeness, a walled set of values and the crème de la crème! A notable example is the Ten Commandments in the Bible, a set of principles and life values that have shaped culture, history and the laws of nations to this day.

I wanted to distil into ten key areas those principles, values, strategies and tactics that have helped shape the destinies of the hundreds of clients that we have worked with over the last twenty years. As in all things, we cannot guarantee success, but we are incredibly confident that growth will result, as denoted by our clients who have grown significantly in an economic environment that is unprecedented in modern times. These folks have made us look good, and we are grateful that their hard work and trust in the new strategic direction and business culture we proposed to them has revolutionised their businesses.

It is important to state that these ten commandments operate within the organisation of every business at various levels. Our strength has been to unlock the hidden potential in a business, use these commandments to mend what is broken, and to accelerate understanding, execution and, ultimately, growth.

There will be other 'commandments' that you may deem important, and we're not disagreeing with them. All we have attempted to do is to present those that have had the biggest impact on our clients in terms of return on investment.

The final point to mention is the power of leadership in executing these commandments. The leader needs to practise and exemplify these principles on a day-to-day basis. The passion needs to permeate from the executive team through management to those at the front line. For us, engaging employees in the strategic direction and execution of business goals is the number one activity that unlocks the potential of a business.

In a world that is racked with uncertainty and fear, especially during this COVID-19 pandemic, our hope is that these ten commandments will provide the foundation for your business growth. They will enable it not only to survive but to be part of the next generation of businesses that lead their market, benefit their sector and impact positively on society.

We would love to talk with you about how these ten commandments can impact your business, so please do not hesitate to contact us on letstalk@10bizcommandments.com

1

Thou shalt create a clear vision for the growth of the business.

In ancient times, King Solomon understood the power of having a strong vision for the people of Israel. To ensure this, he enshrined his words in print: 'without Vision the people cast off restraint'.[i] He was clear that, without a vision, people are like sheep without direction or hope.

Today, the slogans '*Every little helps*' from Tesco, and '*Never knowingly undersold*' from John Lewis, communicate to customers – and importantly staff – the values and the core aspects of their vision. Tom Shoes is a great example of tying in a vision with their customers: for each pair of designer shoes a customer buys, another pair is sent free to a country or village where shoes are needed. [ii]

Vision inspires confidence - it sets the scene for what can be achieved and gives us the strength to carry on when our circumstances are far from that desired future. In these unprecedented times, we need business leaders to have a strong vision to carry and propel their businesses forward.

So how does one create a compelling business vision?

Produce a headline vision statement or future intent

It is important to project where you see your business in the future. Think of the future in three-year periods. Three years is a good target; you will have a feel for the marketplace and its changes over the next twelve to twenty-four months, but typically nobody knows what is going to happen in three years' time! This process allows you to update your vision on a yearly basis and test your three-year plan.

- Think about what the business should focus on (products or services).
- What sectors and territories are you likely to be involved in?
- What type of customers are you likely to serve, or want to serve?
- How will you communicate with them? Using traditional ways, through a sales team and direct marketing, or by using the internet and social media platforms – or both?
- Think about the turnover, profitability and margin that you would expect to achieve in three years.

- Visualise the people who are driving the business. What talent do you need to support its growth?
- Does your business have the appropriate systems in place to measure the growth that you achieve? Can you monitor 'timely' performance in every part of the business?
- Do you have the cashflow to fuel the growth in people, products and systems? If not, what do you need to achieve the success you want? Identifying this is the most important first step to take *before* talking to the bank, business angels or venture capitalists.
- The pointers listed above are essential components of a business plan. However, my 'beef' with producing a business plan is that the process results in a document without a soul, and invariably it is quickly forgotten once funding has been obtained.

The power of breaking down the vision into strategic themes

The approach I take in my business is to identify an understanding of the strategic themes that will allow the business to grow and develop, from the initial vision of turnover and profitability after three years. The case study at the end of this chapter illustrates an example of this approach. The strategic themes are important because they form a rung on the business growth ladder, where each step is important for the company to achieve its goals.

In our strategy sessions with clients, we normally identify between twelve and sixteen strategic themes that the company needs to execute to achieve the growth to which it aspires. However, it is usually clear that, with its current team, cash resources and systems etc., the client company does not have the capacity to do them all. Our approach, therefore, is to work with the senior executive team to identify and prioritise a core number of themes (three to five of them) that can be carried out with the available resources as a means of kick-starting the growth strategy.

The power of this process only becomes evident when engagement with staff takes centre stage; they must also understand the plan and their role in executing the goals of the business. Whereas a business plan may only be shared with a privileged few, the vision and the strategic themes are shared with everyone in the business to harness engagement and ownership of the growth plan.

The themes are then broken down into 'projects', which have clear objectives, plans, timescales, goals and ownership. This allows a clear visual and documented map of how the company will achieve its goals and who is involved in that achievement.

It goes without saying that the communication process should be fluid, with managers regularly reporting the progress of the projects to the owner of the strategic theme (typically an executive). Additional quarterly updates by the MD or CEO will help staff understand the impact that their own work is having on the strategic theme goals and the overall goals of the organisation.

This process is not just useful in large organisations; small and medium organisations benefit massively from this approach and achieve extraordinary growth. An example of a small company that has done this is illustrated in this case study.

Case Study

AWAKENING THE GIANT - HELPING SCIPAC'S TOP TEAM WIN BIG

Changing the culture and thinking of a major business within fifteen months to achieve a 40% growth in revenue and a 60% increase in profit for the financial year ending March 2009 took some doing. However, Scipac's tenacity in implementing our growth strategies at all levels of the business was key to these dramatic results.

Scipac (now part of the BBI Group) had been trading for nearly thirty years. Started by Dr Clive Dawes and the late Tony Raeside, it has developed a range of innovative products that are used in the health diagnostic sector.

After twenty-three years, the business had reached a performance plateau. There had been a failed takeover attempt, and the management team was fragmented and underperforming. Bruce Corp, who was then the finance director, took over the managing director's role in order to stabilise the business and restore profitability before his retirement. Stephane Argivier, the young sales director, was being groomed to become managing director.

Scipac understood that a strategy away-day with Bruce and Stephane would help facilitate thinking about the organisation's vision and direction for the next three-year period, and help them create a model with practical steps to get there. For the organisers of the away-day, part of that process was to help Scipac visualise what could be achieved in three to five years, to understand the type of customers that it could do business with, and to consider what territories it could work in. In addition, the strategy session reviewed the products or innovations that were driving sales, the operations that underpinned services, and the financial models that would maintain growth.

Scipac had just completed the first year of its five-year strategic plan and experienced some growth, but Bruce and Stephane felt that an independent review could help to unlock the business's growth and potential. For Stephane Argivier, the managing director elect, it was clear that the pace of change had to be much quicker in order to keep up with the market place and 'to get relevant experience into the management team as fast as possible'.

From the strategy session, Bruce and Stephane prioritised three strategic themes that they believed would unlock the potential of the business. These were: quality; faster innovation culture; and improving the skills capability of the top team to facilitate growth and the engagement of the staff in line with the strategy.

The solutions to these themes centred on communicating and reporting to the staff on a regular basis and using the appraisal process to ensure that their work (or objectives) matched the strategic themes and goals.

Following the strategy session, Bruce and Stephane believed that it was important to help the executive team gain the necessary skills to handle the growth of the business. Over six to eight months, a programme of executive coaching support was put in place with the senior management team, to support their skills development.

Executing these three strategic themes meant that three years later Scipac was awarded the 2010 Queen's Award for Export and also for Innovation. It is very rare to obtain two awards. A few years later, it was acquired by BBI Solutions because of its impressive growth.

2

Thou shalt love thy customer as thyself.

Customers are the lifeblood of every business. Loving or hating them is one thing, but losing them could bring your business down!

As we've mentioned before, it is important to understand that customers buy from you to fulfil a need or to solve a problem. It is this tenuous relationship that all organisations must get a handle on. Once a customer no longer sees value in the relationship, services or product, they start to think of you as just a supplier rather than a partner or trusted advisor and they may go elsewhere.

The following graphic is one that I have used in countless business discussions, webinars, business presentations and publications. For me, it simply states the importance of retaining your clients, especially those who contribute most to your revenue and, more importantly, your profits.

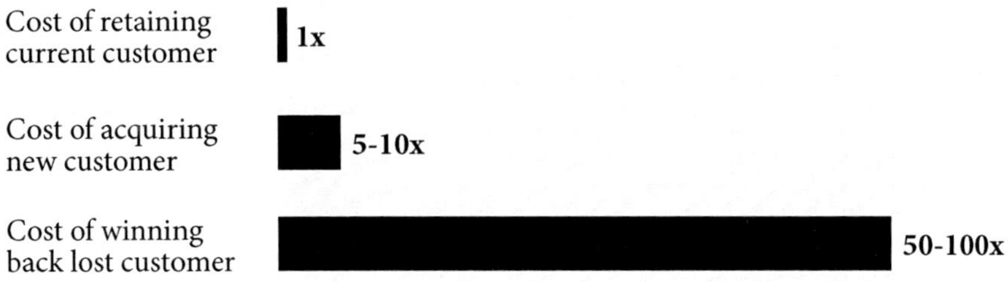

Rob Yanker, former partner of McKinsey & Company, produced this graphic to demonstrate the cost of acquiring, maintaining and losing a customer. What is most striking is the cost of acquiring a new client (i.e., the effort involved in marketing and sales activity). The other striking feature here is the cost of regaining a client. Put simply, it is fifty to one hundred times more costly to try to regain an old client than to gain a new one. So, the big learning point here is look after your existing clients at all times.

How do we do this? I am glad you asked this question. Before we answer it, consider the reasons why clients leave a business.

- They are fed up with poor customer service.
- They are fed up with poor quality products.
- They are fed up with continual poor delivery of services and products.
- There is a relationship breakdown between the key buyer and the representative of your business.
- The key buyer moves on and their replacement chooses his/her preferred supplier.
- There is an inability to meet ongoing or future demand for services and products.
- The company gets taken over by a larger group that has its own preferred supplier.

An important point needs to be emphasised here. Being a supplier means that you may be one of many routes for your customer to fulfil their business objectives. If this is so, your value may be diminished because similar services can be obtained from your competitors. Your goal as a business is to become a business supply *partner* to your customers, offering an indispensable service that they rely on. To most businesses, becoming a supply partner means that you are an integral part of their business strategy, processes and procedures. An example is Ocado, which is the home delivery partner of Waitrose and Morrisons.

Becoming indispensable to your customers is an important element of your business, but business growth is predicated on keeping existing clients happy and adding to the 'client pot'. Losing clients is like having a leaking bucket: it never becomes full because the rate of water loss is equal to, or more than, the amount of water topping up the bucket.

So, here are a number of tips to ensure that you lay the foundation for securing and retaining happy customers.

Evaluate internally how you see your clients

Evaluate a list of your key customers and decide whether they are at risk of leaving the business. Rank them on a scale of 1–5 (1 being least likely). If any show values of 3 to 5, then devise strategies to bring them down to 1. As we said before, spending money to move the client down to 1 or 2 is cheaper than either acquiring a new client or trying to regain the old client – or, at worst, losing the client altogether.

Talk to them!

When was the last time you talked to your clients about your performance? If possible, carry out an external customer satisfaction review and share the findings with your clients. Highlight the good things that you do, then outline key actions and timelines to correct poor or average performance.

Find out what delights or excites clients about your product or service.

This is the one area that I guarantee (if you get it right) will lead to more business or a stronger relationship. Remember, the customer first bought from you because you had addressed a need or 'pain' that they had. Finding out whether you are still pressing the same relationship buttons is essential. If you are not, you could become another 'supplier' rather than a supply partner. If there is no value in the relationship then the client is likely to move to a competitor because of price rather than value.

Find out their three-year business strategic plan and partner them in that plan

You may say that it's none of your business but, if you can add value by helping clients to execute their strategic vision, this will cement you as an important partner rather than just another supplier. An example of this is helping the customer to launch a new product or service in a new territory or marketplace. This knowledge may mean that you have to plan for your own investment in plant or customer/technical service to support any product launches that your client may undertake.

Do not argue if there is a problem!

It is easy to blame the client or not respond in a crisis - for example, a perceived product 'failure', a service gone wrong or incorrect documentation. The key thing in these instances is to immediately correct the problem as if it were your fault, then carry out a clear objective-based investigation in a timely manner using one of your senior people. Discuss the findings with the customer and outline any steps (on both sides) to prevent the issue reoccurring. This could make or break a business. Get the process wrong by not responding correctly on in a timely manner and you could lose a valuable client. Get it right, and you will create the strong perception that you're not just a supplier but a partner willing to respond to any situation.

Be grateful and say thank you often

Never assume that your client 'owes' you for letting them purchase your product over the last one, two or even fifty years! You have no right to their business, and your humble approach will ensure that you have a long and lasting relationship. Offer incentives, gifts, timely discounts on product prices – anything that tells the client that you are grateful for their business.

This growth commandment is one that features strongly with all our successful clients. The treatment of customers is only a reflection of how you would like your own suppliers to treat you. If you expect shoddy treatment and poor service, it is likely that you will give it to your customers too.

Case Study

(CLIENT NAME CHANGED TO MAINTAIN CONFIDENTIALITY)

Malcolm Food Solutions Ltd is the market leader in providing innovative product formulations for the food industry, using ingredients that help give ready-made foods a high sheen and good texture. From day one, the company has always prized itself on responding to customer needs. Dealing with market leaders in a billion-dollar industry requires a degree of flexibility and technical knowledge to evaluate needs, recommend a range of solutions, and to scale up if trials go well. Quality is critical, and a systematic process is in place to ensure that each batch is fully identifiable from base formulation to finished goods. Any complaints are dealt with swiftly and effectively because the company keeps samples of key batches for future reference in the event of product issues.

However, in a price-sensitive marketplace, Malcolm Food Solutions needed to firm up relationships with its customers by offering them longer-term contracts. They achieved this by investing financially in partnerships with growers of raw materials who were responsible for providing the base materials used in food products. By securing long-term contracts with the growers, Malcolm Food Solutions could provide the same supply-chain partnership assurances to their clients and secure product pricing with their customers as a means of locking out their competitors. This left the competitors with a shortage of base raw materials and resulted in them having to offer higher prices to maintain profitability. Maintaining the volume of sales meant that the Malcolm Food Solutions manufacturing plant could improve running costs and margins and increase the profitability of the business as a low manufacturing cost business.

Why was this focus on the supply chain important for Malcolm Food Solutions? Well, the company knew from their discussions with customers, that a faster response to their customers' raw materials supply need would benefit and delight them. In addition, continuity of supply and of price was essential for their customers' profitability when negotiating with supermarkets. By focussing on the supply chain, Malcolm Food Solutions immediately became the preferred supplier and partner for many of the industry's leading global food producers. With its unrivalled innovative ability to support new customer products, this has helped to double the size of the business over the last eight years.

3

Thou shalt create a pipeline of sales opportunities.

We have already discussed the importance of delighting and looking after your customers; now I would like to look at the increasingly important process of acquiring customers. Sales are the fuel which drives a business forward. Without sales, the business stutters and dies. With the advent of doing business via the internet and the increasing importance of social media to drive sales, businesses need to be agile and flexible in finding new ways to acquire and communicate with new customers.

This chapter focuses on the processes and systems for customer acquisition rather than the sales skill of converting prospects into buying customers. There are many good books on this subject – but not so many on the process of cultivating and acquiring new clients.

System focus

In order to capture potential clients, there must be a system to collate information about them. We're assuming that you are clear about the type of clients that demand your product or service so there is not a scatter-gun approach to identifying those prospective clients. Focus is an essential element of the sales hunter.

Customer relationship management (CRM) systems are huge software databases that allow a company or organisation to collate key information about a customer so as to understand their needs, buying patterns and key contacts within the organisation. This repository of data is essential because it means that reports can be generated to highlight the needs of the client, who in the organisation has contacted them, products that they buy, etc.

Many organisations also use CRM systems to track prospective clients through the sales process, from initial contact through to proposal, then on to final closing of the sale. This process is extremely powerful and helps the salesperson to understand how effectively they generate sales. The more sophisticated CRM products can also link emails, reports, legal documents, voice recordings and videos to the client.

Why do I mention this? Well, the importance of understanding your clients and their needs in real time is becoming increasingly important, not only to keep the client (account management function) but also to stay ahead of competitors who are all too ready to take your client from under your nose.

Remember that we discussed the importance of keeping your customers and growing your business on the back of existing clients? This fact alone should be enough to make you consider employing more relevant systems.

Offline customer acquisition strategies

The traditional way of acquiring customers is through direct marketing, such as telephoning (cold calling) and mailing / emailing prospective customers. Although its use is not as prevalent today in the majority of businesses, this still has tremendous benefits; indeed, in many quarters it is seen as 'the' new marketing tool for brand awareness and customer acquisition. Ironically, because 'junk' or advertising mail through the post has become less commonplace, it is now more likely that we will look at it compared to fifteen years ago.

This, therefore, provides a fantastic opportunity to present your proposition, as well as linking up with the new opportunities that the internet and social media provide in showcasing products and services.

Online customer acquisition strategies

Without question, the internet and the advent of social media have changed the game for many businesses. Being able to contact and acquire customers from anywhere in the world at the click of a button has created, as well as decimated, many a business.

The inability of the UK electrical store Comet to implement an online strategic sales portal to support its sales in the retail store contributed to its demise in 2012. This illustrates the need for businesses to be agile; they should not assume that their business model will survive.

Other examples of this are department stores like M&S, BHS or House of Fraser, which are being hammered by nimble and innovative online fashion and household goods organisations like Asos, Boohoo, Wayfair and Made.com. As we have mentioned before, it is critical that organisations understand the 'why' of what customers want from them. These organisations have failed to understand the changing landscape and needs of their clients.

Tesco consolidated its market position, improving innovation for, and understanding of, its customers following the success of its Club Card campaign. It was the first supermarket to have an online buying portal, well before broadband was prevalent around the UK. I remember ordering the shopping for my wife, who was too busy looking after our three small children; I still recall the frustration of dealing with a flaky dial-up system and the joy of seeing the order being accepted. One could argue that getting in the car and shopping in the store would have been quicker. Many times, it was! But this process not only solidified my relationship with Tesco but made me into a 'Tesco evangelist', telling my friends about this new software approach to shopping.

This leads me nicely on to discussing the power of social media in acquiring customers. The advent of Facebook, LinkedIn, Twitter, Instagram, TikTok, Trip Advisor, Trust Pilot and other social-media portals has created huge communities that provide information on a variety of topics, products and companies. Here are two examples of the power of these portals to engage prospective clients.

LinkedIn is an online portal for business professionals where they can upload the basic details of their CV in a format that allows them not only to attract potential new job opportunities but to extol the virtues of their business. Additional features of LinkedIn include interest groups around a key topic (for example, Innovation Group) which allows individuals to engage in discussions about activities, changes in legislation, new ideas, etc. Engaging in the right forum and establishing expert credentials through thoughtful blog posts can be a useful way of engaging a new client.

An example of how this type of forum can generate business occurred in my organisation. I had engaged in a discussion online with a prospective customer. It resulted in me providing them with a relevant answer to a question. This was followed offline with a face-to-face meeting to establish more of their business needs. Through further discussions, we were able to outline a business proposal, which the new client accepted, to move the business to the next level of growth.

Another example is the power of association. LinkedIn encourages you to link to other professionals that you know and value. We had a client who was struggling to contact someone from Thames Water. I had a strong relationship with someone from Scottish Gas and noticed that he had a similar relationship with someone in Thames Water. My Scottish Gas contact introduced me to his Thames Water contact, who eventually contacted his local director and put me in contact with the operational manager at the local Thames Water centre. The process took twenty-four hours! Because my colleague at Scottish Gas was a valued contact of the senior executive, this executive trusted his judgement, which in turn meant that I could also be trusted to add value. To enable this relationship to happen using cold calling would have been impossible within these timescales. Social media, rather than the traditional email blast or direct mail, provides the opportunity to target the customers you want anywhere in the world.

However, the advent of the internet and social media has also put a massive spotlight on the importance of protecting the reputation of your business. If your sales and acquisition tactics are questionable, this is likely to be broadcast very quickly. Trip Advisor and Twitter are examples of social media platforms that have caused much pain and reputation meltdown to companies, organisations and individuals who do not operate or behave appropriately. The world is a different place and it has become very difficult to hide!

Case Study

Influential Software is a business focussed on providing business intelligence software and bespoke software process solutions to the finance, insurance and publishing sectors. When we met with the key executives it was clear that, although their business was very profitable, their reliance on one client who contributed 90% of their revenue to a multimillion-pound business was a tenuous situation.

We helped them think through a clear action plan for client acquisition, focusing on creating a solid CRM (in this case using Salesforce[iii]) and systematically targeting clients through their website, social media and the normal sales channel processes.

The results were impressive, especially considering there was a downturn in the marketplace. Turnover increased by a multiple of four, and reliance on this key client for revenue and profitability was reduced dramatically to 60% within eighteen months and 30% in three years. Opportunities were created with similar size clients to the existing key one, leading to a strong prospect of future growth. In addition, the number of prospective leads that were generated started to pose additional problems to the business in finding resources and time to follow them through. Through a number of acquisitions, the resources to deal with this aspect have been realised.

4

Thou shalt market the business continually - but be humble about it!

In any business growth strategy, the principles of marketing will underpin that growth. Word of mouth, or sales that are derived as a result of customers talking to other prospective customers, are incredibly important and will certainly take the business to a greater level of success. However, a business that wants to dominate its market sector must have in place systematic processes and systems for sales and marketing.

Definition of marketing: '*...the action or business of promoting and selling products or services, including market research and advertising*' [iv]

Books about marketing abound but the problem with these self-help manuals is that, at times, they fail to integrate marketing with an overall business strategy. Marketing will impact every aspect of the business because it communicates the values and culture of the business, the products' features and benefits, and positions the company's brand and its products in a way that differentiates it from others. Consequently, it is essential that any marketing plan is integrated with every (note, I said *every*) function of the business.

A good example of this is the impact of marketing on the finance part of a business. This may seem nebulous, but why not take the opportunity to reinforce the company's brand values on invoices, or mention a promotion on Facebook, Twitter or web links? The point is that marketing activity should seek to communicate with customers at all times, as well as reinforcing the culture and branding internally. It seems sensible to use every opportunity to do so.

It would not surprise me if a new social media platform comes into play before this book is published. The rise of Twitter is testimony of the power of communication. It is said that the BBC, the premier broadcaster in the UK, now communicates its breaking news over Twitter before it broadcasts it on TV, radio or its internet site. The speed of information, and the willingness of individuals to expose the intricacies of their lives, can be a benefit as well as a business risk to a company that embraces these communication tools. Our example, in a subsequent, chapter discusses launching the new Pfizer Chapstick product on Facebook as an example of the importance of using marketing effectively, as well as managing negative responses in an appropriate way.

An example of the strategic marketing plan that we adopt with our clients is known as the 5W strategic model.

5W strategic model

The 5W strategic model has been created to take organisations through a step-by-step process to create, execute and review strategic plans in real time. The process follows the 'Plan/Do/Check/Act' philosophy that many management organisations have used to create process improvements for companies.

The strategic model can be represented graphically by the 5W wheel. We will consider each area in turn.

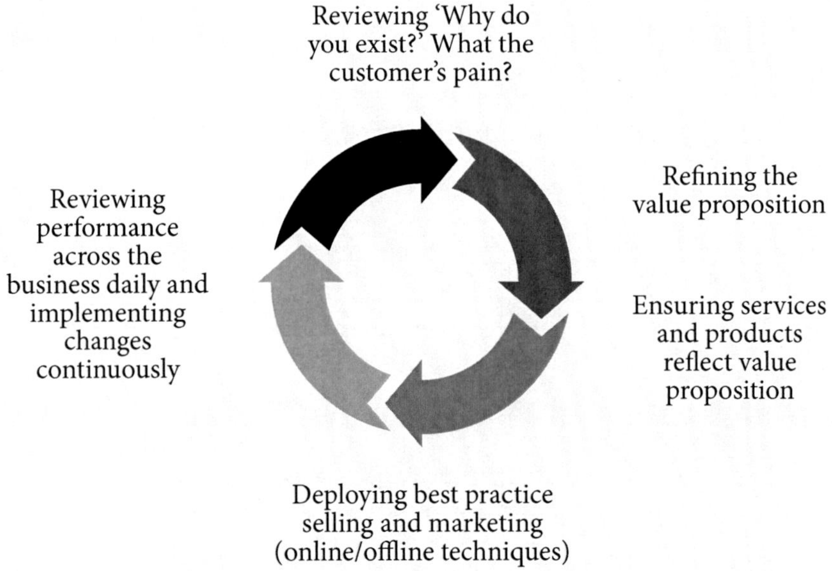

Reviewing *'Why do you exist?'* What is the customer's pain?

It's important to get this part of the marketing strategy process right because it answers the question of why you are in business. Why do customers buy from you? What makes customers buy from you rather than your competitors?

Getting to the root of this question helps to establish whether:

- your product and services are relevant to the market today
- your sales literature reflects the needs of your customers
- your customer service practices are in line with your original values.

How do you collate this information? Well, find out from your customers and suppliers by talking to them directly. Let them be candid with you and tell you, warts and all, about the products and services that you provide. You will be horrified by some things, but I guarantee that you will be delighted by others.

Kodak had to redefine their business using this approach so that they could capitalise on the market for digital cameras rather than photographic film – but they were too late! M&S had to go back to their core values in order to arrest declining sales in food, women's clothing and underwear. Some commentators believe they are too late to arrest the decline.

Refining the value proposition

Distilling the key attributes of what makes the business unique is the domain of the creative marketing people in your business. Needless to say, a strapline that defines the heart of the business can be a compelling message to the marketplace not only of your intent, but also as a means of describing the 'soul' or 'heart' of the business.

One word of caution: it is incredibly important that, if you have a culture that defines your values as 'delighting your customers', 'ethical in our relationships with customers, suppliers and staff', etc., that you make it clear and prescriptive what that means. Many an organisation has used its culture mantra to emphasise to the world how they want to do business, but has been tested and found wanting. An example is Google's 'never do evil' company mantra being derided in the press when they are seen to be too aggressive with new entrants or other organisations[v]. Your business reputation is incredibly important. We look at culture and ethics later in this book.

Ensuring services and products reflect the value proposition

Once you understand the culture and values that make your business successful, communicate them to the marketplace, your suppliers and across the business. However, it is essential that your company embraces this *before* you communicate to the marketplace. Ensure that every process and procedure captures the essence of the business. If it is about a quality product, tell your audience about the processes that you use to define and excel in quality. If it is about design, define how your design is unique. Never knock the competition, but always trumpet your product, services and people.

One area that we thoroughly recommend, is ensuring employees have their work objectives linked to the overall strategy of the business. Use the appraisal process to do this. In companies that we've worked with, a central plank that has driven business growth and success is when employees understand their impact on the overall strategic direction of the business and have goals that link to the overall goals of the business.

Deploying best practice selling/marketing (online/offline) techniques

Once your internal processes embrace your value proposition, you are ready to communicate to the world. Every medium – direct mail, email, your customer service team, web, social media sites – should communicate the proposition exactly and succinctly.

Reviewing performance across the business daily and implementing changes continuously

The final piece of the puzzle of implementing marketing strategy is to measure the key values and attributes of the business on a regular basis. This ensures that the value proposition is creating maximum value for the business (profits) and customers (customer satisfaction and delight). Use this phase to gain customers' and suppliers' reviews of your business and to find out what delights them. Measure those elements to ensure that you maintain the core values that will help answer the question 'Why do you exist?'.

Case Study

One of my business activities used this approach to marketing successfully. Our business advisory business was built on the following 'customer pain' in the market:

- Companies were fed up with poor advice given by 'business advisors' who had no experience of running a business.
- They did not know where to turn to, other than their accountants who did not have the breadth of experience in running a business except for understanding 'the numbers'.

By focusing on 'Why should customers call upon a business advisor?' it was easy to identify those clients who:

- wanted advisors who knew how to run or turn around businesses – who already had the T-shirt!
- did not want to be told what to do, but wanted someone to teach them to think in the right way to drive the business forward
- could call upon clients that had been with us and demonstrated substantial business growth.

We also identified those clients by looking at online postings and reviewing financial company standing from Companies House.

By using free postings on LinkedIn, blog posts and direct-mail marketing literature, we highlighted our work with clients who fitted our service profile. Testimonies and feedback from clients were essential in ensuring that we met their needs and delighted them.

In addition, we have a systematic approach to keeping in contact with clients long after we have completed contracted work. This ensures longevity of relationships and, in many cases, additional work with other members of the business as the company grows.

This ongoing discussion with clients informs us if we are still relevant to the marketplace and so meets our question of 'Why should we exist as a business?'.

5

Thou shall create an innovation culture.

Innovation is the use of new or different ideas or methods to create better or more effective products, processes, services, technologies or ideas that are accepted by markets, governments and society. This is different to invention, which refers more directly to the creation of a brand-new idea, product or method.

The power of innovation is very clear in our society. The impact of Apple's dominance in the marketplace is not its invention of new products but its innovation and repackaging of ideas that were already in the marketplace. When Steve Jobs came back to Apple as CEO in the 90s, we saw a shift in the culture to create core values around exceptional design and functionality that 'wowed' customers. Indeed, Apple was able to take advantage of a company that failed to do this. The Palm range of PDAs (Personal Digital Assistants) revolutionised the use of digital interfaces for storing calendar information and files using a touch screen. However, because the manufacturers took their eyes off their core business and entered the world of the smartphone in the mid-2000s, it was badly trounced by Blackberry who created a device that was smaller and allowed the rapid sending and receipt of emails; it was a Palm Treo look alike. But Apple focused on innovation and seized its chance to develop and repackage touch-screen technology to create the iPhone; the rest is history.

Jim Collins in his book *How the Mighty Fall* [vi], presents the concept of 'Hubris Born of Success', where he outlines how companies forget to develop and innovate their core business and go looking for the next 'shiny' product or market opportunity. It is easy to look at your competitors and copy them, rather than to look at ways of innovating your own product line to keep you one step ahead of your competitors.

So how does one create an innovation culture? There is a plethora of books on the subject and some are a worthwhile read. However, we will outline some of the key features of those companies that have realigned their business to become innovation focussed.

Continuous improvement for all activities

This is a culture where processes and activities are continually refined and improved. This is typically not done in isolation but with a team of people from all parts of the organisation. The philosophy is that two heads are better than one and that great ideas can come from people who are outside your area of expertise.

An example is the development of a new product or service that involves your colleagues from each area of the business. Production, quality, marketing, sales and even finance can impact on how the product or service is developed and how it penetrates the market. Identifying new ways of completing a task, manufacturing products, communicating to customers or delivering a product in a different way could have a dramatic impact on the business and its profitability.

Innovate your existing product

As we've said before, it is the focus on developing your core product that will ensure the continuance of its growth cycle. The best way to do this is to develop additional value so that the customer will buy again. This is true for mobile phones, cars and electronic appliances, where different features are packaged up in the next release or range extension. Dyson is very clever at doing this. All of its products have the same suction performance but designing and marketing it in different ways for different sectors (car cleaning or wooden floors) creates range extensions which will keep the brand and the product alive for many generations. Their current innovation focus on working with battery technology for cordless products has helped them to maintain their market share against competitors.

Keeping close to customers will stimulate innovation

Innovation seeks to meet problems head on with solutions. Keeping close to customers will help you identify the issues or pain they are experiencing. If you can come up with a solution to address this, you will have a product or service that is of value.

Many of the top businesses call in their technical or operational personnel to support a sales call as a way of not only staying close to customers but supporting those clients with technical resources to resolve any difficulties that they have. This is because someone who is 'non-salesy' can ask questions and see things in a different light to those who are trained in sales. In such a meeting, the technical individual can look for opportunities that the customer or the sales individual may not have noticed.

In addition, a strong customer service or sales function will ask questions such as: 'Are you experiencing any problems with our product or service?' or 'What can we do to improve any issues that you may be experiencing?' This approach to keeping close to customers provides the information that, if collated in the organisation, could foster new approaches and ideas to meet the needs of not only one customer but many. Keeping close to customers can stimulate the creation of innovative solutions, products or services, which will (in our experience) always command higher margins in relation to competitors.

Case Study

PetroTechnik is a company that was started in 1991 to capitalise on the need for the replacement of underground steel pipework in the petroleum forecourt marketplace. Environmental pressure by local government on oil companies had reached fever pitch, with many petrol forecourts experiencing massive contamination and receiving large clean-up bills because of leaking underground pipework and tanks.

John Boudry, the then CEO, identified an opportunity in the marketplace for a product that could reduce site installation times by at least 50% while improving the quality of dispensing petrol and diesel, as well as giving excellent customer service. The UPP product range was born. With the clever use of manufacturers to make the products, the company could focus on distributing and marketing with the help of a strong sales and marketing team. This fast growth and the introduction of worldwide environmental legislation banning the use of metallic pipework led to the market changing to polymeric pipework systems overnight.

However, by 1996 the company had reached a plateau of performance at a turnover of £6m. Competitors were coming to the fore, and the oil companies were using the threat of new potential suppliers to drive down product prices. In addition, globalisation had hit the industry and the oil companies wanted product agreements for 'identical products' at a unique sales price, distributed to its sites worldwide irrespective of currency fluctuations. PetroTechnik had operations in UK, France and Australia and knew that this would not be enough, especially for the emerging markets and that graveyard of British companies, the USA.

Three strategic masterstrokes saved the business. The first was to bring in outside talent to drive the operations and product development functions of the business, as well as creating a board that revolved around John (finance and sales) to allow him more focus on working 'on' the business rather than 'in' it. The new team transformed the business from small to medium sized with the introduction of efficient systems to manage the international nature of the business, better cash treasury management and new supplier agreements, which in one year added £350k to the bottom line.

The second masterstroke was the release of a culture of innovation into the business and the creation of intellectual property (IP) that would add massive goodwill to its value. John Boudry knew that the business was losing its innovative brand tag with a product that was six years old. However, with a clear focus from the board on R&D and a small amount of investment, the new team created seven patents in its first year, leading to innovations that not only cemented the core product sales but also brought into play other products that were poor sellers. Since then, the business had gone on to continually innovate its range and acquired many new patents.

The third masterstroke was to create a business model that protected the company from manufacturers that had similar product capabilities. A pipe-making tool was developed with a Swiss company and delivered under licence to a manufacturing partner in Brazil. This ensured that the quality of the product was consistent, as well as improving the margins of the locally delivered product. Additional manufacturing capability was developed in the USA and China to facilitate the global demand. The globalisation strategy ensured that global agreements could now be competitively priced and delivered with the same excellent service, onsite training and customer service anywhere in the world.

Ten years later, Franklin Energy[vii] I bought the PetroTechnik Group outright for $15m in cash, with the group contributing $40m in sales revenue to Franklin Energy [vii]. The key lesson of innovating to protect the core business sales and investing in infrastructure and IP, proved to be the correct growth strategy for PetroTechnik.

Apart from a few companies, this is a strategy that we have lost in the UK. Anybody can acquire businesses and cut costs to drive profitability. However, it is only innovative products that will add greater margins and profits for a company, as well as maintaining or growing market share.

6

Thou shalt understand the 'numbers' or die.

If you have been in business for any length of time, you will have heard the mantra that 'revenue is vanity, profit is reality and cash is king'. There is real truth to this statement and it is worth understanding each one of the terms.

Revenue

Revenue is important as it helps position the business differently in the eyes of suppliers and customers alike, both in a good and in a bad sense. The good sense is that the negotiating power of the business is enhanced for purchasing raw materials and products, and the clients' perception is that the business is financially stronger because it is bigger by virtue of turnover. In addition, due to the risk-averse nature of public-sector authorities, the perception is that larger companies 'supposedly' have deeper pockets to negate any issues around lack of supply, failure or other adverse developments. The stock market clearly is affected (unfortunately in my view) by revenue as an indicator of a company's growth although, in a recessionary environment, market share and profit should be the overall indicator of growth.

It is frightening how often I hear business owners say that they would like to reach £1m turnover, £10m turnover, £300m turnover, as if this number helps them to define themselves or their business. 'I run a £300m business' is a vanity statement. The statement does not define the health and strength of the business or its future viability, as proven by many large businesses with high turnovers that have gone bust (Enron, Lehman Brothers, Woolworths, Kodak, Curry's, Karen Millen and Clintons Cards in the UK are notable examples). However, although revenue growth is important, it is only part of the equation of what makes a sustainable and successful business.

Profit

Profit is an essential element of a business because it allows the creation of cash for reinvestment and/or to pay shareholders on their initial and ongoing investment in the company. Not enough organisations consider this an important aspect of the day-to-day running of the business. Our work with companies always takes business leaders back to this one question: 'How do you know if you are making money on this product or service?'

When reviewing the profit of a service or product, one must be cognisant of all the cost elements in producing and selling the product and the expenses incurred in selling and delivering a service. In our experience, this basic management information is not readily available in a good proportion of businesses. The way we help businesses to understand profit is to work with them on the 'profit-levers' in their business. In other words, we look at the key activities or aspects that have the biggest impact on the profitability of the service or product. Examples include:

- raw material costs
- packaging costs
- manufacturing, logistics and quality control costs (especially those involving high use of fuels)
- labour rates increases through unionised or government =legislative activities
- competitor activity e.g. discounting or new products introduction
- commoditised product range
- increased costs through personnel acquisition or other marketing activities (such as traditional and social media channels).

By understanding the key profit levers of a business, one can set up performance metrics to monitor their changes over a period of time. In addition, a number of strategies and tactics can be created to minimise their impact on profitability.

Understanding the profit levers allows the business to react to market demands or new product entries. This allows a good benchmark for the comparison of the products and services against competitors.

A better understanding of the costs of a product and service will ensure that these make a profit rather than a loss for tendered activities. One can also make a judgement on whether one product range or service is more profitable than another and allow for adjustment of marketing spend to help improve or boost a flagging sales activity.

This analysis is incredibly important. We have known businesses that have celebrated with Champagne after winning a large tender, only to realise later that the tender was unprofitable, putting the business in financial jeopardy.

Profit provides the engine for the creation of cash in the business. If an activity is loss-making then no cash is generated, leading to the use of cash reserves to sustain the business. A depletion of cash reserves will cause a business to go bust, even if turnover is high.

Cash

The importance of cash management cannot be overstated. All businesses fail for the simple reason that they run out of cash. The issues leading to this are different for each business, but the result is the same: once you have run out of cash, you are not in a position to pay suppliers for raw materials, run the manufacturing plant, pay your staff, and service any other debts that you may have accrued.

There are plenty of books designed to help owners understand the importance of cash management, but we have outlined below a number of key principles that we consider are important to understand and to monitor on a regular basis, in order to ensure a healthy cash position is created in an organisation.

- Invoice immediately – do not wait days/weeks/months to invoice a client.
- Collect cash assertively – you are better off with money in your bank rather than in someone else's!
- Minimise the debtors who are due over and above their payment terms and have a process to communicate and to encourage payment, such as staged payment, early settlement reductions, posting invoice reminder letters in brown envelopes!
- In our opinion, factoring debts (where a company sells its invoices to a third party in return for instant cash to a percentage of the invoice value) should be the last, last, last resort. Very few companies get out of factoring once they have started and it is normally the slippery road to business failure.

- Pay suppliers on time. If you are going to be late, suggest a suitable plan that they can support you with. Treat them as you would like your customers to treat you!
- Forecast cashflow regularly; this will help you to curb spending and prevent a false sense of security from looking at what is currently showing on the bank balance

From the above, I hope it is easy to see that a focus on maintaining a healthy profit as the business grows will provide the cash to sustain growth as well as to invest in marketing and R&D. However, a firm grasp and monitoring of all activities to manage the cashflow throughout the business is essential for the long-term stability of the business.

Cash injection for growth

There are many financial solutions for getting cash into the business and many books on the subject. An example is the *Good Finance Guide for Small Businesses: How to Raise, Manage and Grow your Company's Cash.*[viii] This is a good start but needs to be updated to encompass other funding streams, such as crowdfunding platforms like Crowdcube, Seedrs or Funding Circle. I do not want to go into detail but to highlight that, as long as you have created a solid platform for the business and understand the key profit levers that drive margins and cash, it will be easier to obtain funding from a range of sources – even banks that invariably look for personal guarantees to complement loans and overdraft facilities.

Case Study 1

Paul Henry Architects Ltd (PHA) is one of the leading architectural practices within East London. Whilst many UK architects have hit the wall during the recession, PHA's understanding of key financial profit levers in the business have allowed it to weather the storm and position itself effectively for growth, once the recession in the construction sector ended.

Part of the practice's focus is to ensure that each job makes a profit. This is achieved by:

- involving the team in quotations, which allows the accurate costing of jobs
- managing the execution process of the work effectively so that the project is completed on time
- reviewing the cost base of the business yearly (break even) to ensure that revenue from projects covers overheads as well as contributing to profit
- focusing on selling services on value rather than cost as a means of preserving margins and profitability.

As a result of these practices, the business has stabilised in revenue and gained market share in some areas. The cash management processes, such as staged payments within projects and staged payment of invoices, have all helped massively to ensure that the business keeps its debtor levels manageable and sustainable, thus boosting cash flow. More importantly, this agile approach ensured the company was in the best position to drive growth following changes put in place to protect the business.

Case Study 2

GPC Clear Solutions Ltd is one of the leading organisations for providing innovative water treatment solutions to a range of industries and sectors where the control of fluids and slurries are essential.

From the early days, cash management has been key for this small business. Negotiating credit terms and cash settlement strategies have enabled the business to grow and move several times to accommodate its growing needs.

However, this continued growth led to the need for a cash injection to keep up with an increase in clients and opportunities. A Kent County Council (KCC) Innovation Loan was applied for, which allowed businesses to access regional 0% loans of up to £1m for businesses that had innovative solutions leading to employment within the region. Following discussions with Griff Crouch, the managing director, a clear strategy was formulated to put together a strong business plan highlighting the growth of the business, additional employment and the exciting innovations underpinning this growth. Griff and his team carried off the presentation with aplomb, leading to a unanimous acceptance of the loan proposal by KCC.

There was one sticking point: a loan from the bank was essential to complete the overall deal with KCC. As with all banks, loan decision making has now been taken out of the hands of experienced local business managers and sent to a credit team to review. These faceless 'non-business people' have very little accountability to businesses and even business managers. They make loan decisions based on information the business is not privy to, decisions that are NO or YES. If no, you are not even given a reason why!

Following GPC's application to the bank, the decision was a no. The euphoria of the proposal success was being threatened because the KCC deal was predicated on the bank supporting it. One advantage for GPC was a bank manager who listened to us and was prepared to go back to the credit group to review the case. Following our discussions with GPC and the bank's business manager, we gave him enough financial and market information to go back to the bank's credit group. The biggest thing in GPC's favour was the fact that, although the business had put in financial figures, the updated figures not only showed the business was very prudent in its forecast, but that the actual figures were better than the forecasted ones. The bank manager went to his credit team to argue that their review model was incorrect and, for the first time in a long time, the credit team overturned the decision and gave GPC the green light.

GPC has now moved into new premises and completed their fit-out of offices and new laboratories, which has allowed them to capitalise on sales opportunities in their market.

7

Thou shalt not lie, deceive, or steal from your customers, suppliers or your staff.

'Eighteen per cent,' I cried out, 'only 18%!' In a Gallup Poll, only 18% of the public rated the honesty and ethical standards of business executives as 'high' or 'very high'. [ix]

Why is it that the public perceive that being a successful entrepreneur or business owner means that there must be a degree of duplicity in our business dealings? Or is it that we have all fallen prey to the perception that to be successful in business one has to behave like the character Del Boy in *Only Fools and Horses*, a UK comedy series, or Gordon 'Greed is Good' Gekko in the Hollywood film *Wall Street*. Programmes such as *Dragon's Den* or *The Apprentice* seek to propagate this view of ruthlessness – bend the rules, lie on your CV, etc. In essence, they portray hard-nosed business people who do not have an ounce of emotion and compassion.

When one looks at the detail of this public perception of business executives, a number of facts emerge[x].

- The public would like businesses to treat them fairly and with respect.
- The public largely believe that it is possible for business executives to be ethical and successful.
- The public believe that businesses should impact on society for good (be socially responsible).
- The public think that the media and politicians are in the pockets of big businesses.

The hard facts are all apparent. KPMG estimate that it costs over $100bn a year for North American businesses to deal with ethical problems, including investigating and resolving ethical dilemmas. If one takes into account the one-off BP oil-spill disaster in 2010, which cost the company $42bn[xi], it is easy to see that not following due process, cutting corners or fraudulent business dealings can have a dramatic impact on a business.

I am not here to highlight or to condemn anyone's business practice, but I would caution against the long-term business model that unethical practices can build. In this day and age, a business's brand and reputation are incredibly important. And, with the advent of social media and the instant viral nature of Tweets and Facebook comments, unlawful and unethical practices can be exposed to the whole world in micro-seconds.

Two examples will help to provide some credence to these arguments. Arthur Anderson was undoubtedly one of the top global accounting and audit firms. The Enron collapse and the impact on the reputation of Arthur Anderson was enormous. The news that the company's senior managers and partners had instructed staff to shred any information that could implicate it in the fraudulent behaviour of Enron's executives caused Arthur Anderson's demise and collapse. Coming clean would still have impacted on the business but, by displaying a systemic culture of cover up and fraud throughout the whole organisation, Arthur Anderson ensured that its clients were scared of the reputational backlash of being associated with an 'unethical accounting firm'. Large, publicly listed companies' customers wanted nothing to do with it, which ultimately led to its closure.

The second is a recent example that highlights the power of social media to impact on big organisations. One of Pfizer's businesses, ChapStick, launched a Facebook campaign which did not go too well due to an objection from a number of its customers. AdWeek[xii] gives a blow-by-blow account of how ChapStick demonstrated that deletion and cover ups are not good for your business reputation.

ChapStick posts a weird image on Facebook of a woman, ass in the air, looking for her ChapStick behind a couch. Blogger is disgusted, blogs about it. Blogger tries to reply on Facebook too. ChapStick deletes her comments. Others object to the image. ChapStick deletes their comments. ChapStick's ads with the line "Be heard at Facebook.com/ChapStick" start to look foolish. People keep commenting. ChapStick keeps deleting. People get angry. ChapStick gets worried. The image isn't even that big of a deal—it's ChapStick's reaction to the criticism that galls. "What asses," people say of ChapStick (get it?). People start commenting about why they can't see their old comments. ChapStick can't keep up with all the deleting. Comments are getting through, and they're nasty.

Eventually, Pfizer apologised (sort of). The official Pfizer Twitter account (@pfizer_news) said: The ChapStick ad was not intended to offend anyone & we R pulling it ASAP. Thank you to our ChapStick fans for providing this feedback.

It also apologised on Facebook: *We see that not everyone likes our new ad, and please know that we certainly didn't mean to offend anyone! the post says. Our fans and their voices are at the heart of our new advertising campaign, but we know we don't always get it right. We've removed the image and will share a newer ad with our fans soon!*

It is an example, in business terms, of an 'innocuous' event causing huge PR issues for a company that did not have the systems to manage negative comments about the company or the product.

In this case, there was significant damage to the brand and on sales. But the impact of unethical practices can be huge. Another example is the *News International* 'hacking saga' that led to the closure of the then number-one-selling Sunday newspaper in the UK, *News of the World.*

So, what should one do to create an ethical business culture in an organisation? Here are some tips.

- Focus on looking after your customers. Treat them as you would want your suppliers to treat you.
- Treat your suppliers as partners – negotiations must have a win-win scenario.
- If your staff are your number one asset, treat them as such!
- Ethics costs, so sell on value rather than price.
- Survey your clients and suppliers. Ensure that you are doing what you say you do.
- Have a clear vision and engage your team to execute it (this builds trust).

Case study

Wonderful Creative Agency is a business that has been operational for several years. The executive team value the importance of business ethics in its dealings with staff, suppliers and customers. They take the long-term view of building trust and relationships, rather than the 'quick buck' of the short-term deal. This has meant that they have pulled out of bidding for those contracts where they did not believe they could give adequate service and quality for the money that was on the table.

Wonderful's culture is one of giving. In the early days, the executive team routinely played a part in producing work or giving talks to organisations that could not afford 'London agency type activity'. Dan Maudhub, the managing director, formalised this approach by ensuring his staff did 10% of their work on a charitable and volunteer basis. However, Dan was strict about keeping it to that limit. Wonderful then established their own not-for-profit division, utilising their skills in growing businesses and generating leads to help other not-for-profits on a reduced fee basis, as well as financially supporting projects where possible. Yes, the social responsibility of business ethics can be profitable.

Case Study 2

Willerby Landscapes Ltd is one of the South East's leading commercial landscape designers and construction firms. With the collapse of the building sector from 2008, new work became very scarce. This led to many tenders being lost to companies that just wanted to 'buy' the contract at the lowest price so as to keep their workforce active.

Willerby Landscapes has always been prudent in its cashflow management. It used these difficult times to streamline processes, and to ensure that costs and margins were appropriate and in line with the downward pressures on prices experienced in its marketplace.

Let us look at one such large tender that was lost by Willerby Landscapes as a result of price. Although the Willerby negotiating team tried to be transparent and ethical in their communication with the client about the work and costs, the contract still went to their competitor.

Willerby Landscapes, as usual, asked for feedback on why they were unsuccessful. From that feedback, it was clear that the competitor was not fully truthful with the client on costs and quality, as the bid was significantly below what the Willerby Landscapes had tendered. Willerby Landscapes had a wide understanding of suppliers, material costs and the marketplace, so it became very clear that the competitor had bid very low in an attempt to keep its own workforce active.

Willerby Landscapes took the commercial decision to discuss this with the client; however, the decision had been made and was not reversed. The company had worked hard on the tender and forged what they thought was a strong relationship with this prospective client. So rather than go off in a huff, they calmly said, 'We don't know how your supplier priced up the work, but please be assured that if anything goes awry we have the capabilities and track record to support you.'

The account executive kept in touch with the client on a courtesy basis. Within eight months, Willerby Landscapes was asked to come and take over the work due to the poor standard of workmanship. Not only was this a blessing for the business, but the remedial work created margin and profit in addition to the original tender. It is likely that the competitor also had to pay for Willerby Landscape's remedial costs. It costs you less to do the right thing!

8

Thou shalt value the power of coaching and mentoring your staff and yourself.

Leadership is a lonely role. You sometimes have to make decisions that can make a large proportion of your clients, suppliers and staff feel alienated and also appear to jeopardise the future of the business. However, getting the decision right can not only catapult the business to greater heights, but create a business culture that brings internal and external recognition and success.

Those that are successful usually temper their decision with colleagues who can reason, encourage and support them in the good and the difficult times. In larger companies, this takes the form of a group of non-executives who provide guidance and support to the executive team. These individuals have unique skills in defined disciplines that help to support or add value to the business. In our experience, most non-executives usually do not provide a coaching role to the executive, but instead offer a governance check and balancing role to the board. This, in my view, is very misguided because executives need mentoring and coaching to move the business forward.

For smaller companies, the addition of a non-executive is a luxury that they can ill afford. However, truth be known, a large proportion of business owners would appreciate the opportunity to speak to a seasoned entrepreneur who understands the issues that they face in growing their business.

Before I go on, I want to define the roles of mentor and coach in order to clarify the approach that our business takes in supporting growing businesses.

Mentor

A mentor is someone who provides support to an individual. The mentor can be seen as an experienced sounding board, a provider of moral and spiritual support, and someone who encourages as well as challenges in complex or difficult situations. Invariably, the mentor also unlocks issues by bringing other qualified contacts from his or her networks to support the individual's role and activity.

Coach

A coach is someone who helps an individual to improve his or her performance in areas that they are deemed to be lacking, or in activities where they need to improve. The coach can analyse the circumstances and provide solutions (e.g. how to identify and manage talent in the organisation, or how to take and lead the business to the next level of growth, etc.). In addition, the coach encourages and teaches the individual new skills to carry out their role effectively.

Some people have the skills of being both a mentor and a coach although, in our experience, those who are coaches make good mentors but not the other way around. What is clear is that great leaders need access to individuals who can help them in both those areas.

- The benefits of having a mentor to support your leadership development are clear.
- The mentor provides a confidential outlet in which the leader can vent their frustration about issues and successes.
- The mentor provides a sounding board for the leader to discuss key aspects of moving the business forward, especially in areas where business risks needs to be evaluated.
- The mentor challenges thinking and assumptions around those areas without judgement.
- A true mentor will tell you what you sometimes don't want to hear without fear of losing his or her job or not getting paid.
- A strong mentor can help to open up relationships and sectors that may have been eluding the business for many years.
- A good mentor will invariably link your personal life with business performance to ensure that the two are in perfect balance.
- The benefits of having a coach are just as important.
- Supporting your development as a leader and helping you to understand the qualities that make a successful leader.
- Helping you to define your strengths as a leader and to measure performance.
- Helping and training you to develop the skills and tools to delegate and

to manage your time effectively.

- Providing a clear understanding of how to think strategically and how to find time to carry out, monitor and measure strategic activity.
- Being able to tell you the things that you do not want to hear without fear of losing their job.

As we discussed in the previous chapter, leadership can be learnt; therefore, a good mentor and coach is essential to achieving your own personal as well as business goals more quickly.

From our perspective, we always seek to provide mentors and coaches for our clients and look for the following qualities, attributes and skills.

- The ability to work with the leader without seeking to undermine or take over the business.
- Being able to listen with empathy and recommend a range of appropriate solutions.
- Leading the client to arrive at an honest decision rather than what the mentor or coach believes is appropriate. The leader needs to take ownership of every decision.
- The ability to understand and have experience in the key phases of a business – what it is to start, grow, complete and exit a business.
- Empathy with the leader's business sector
- The ability to bring other credible company partners, individuals and contacts to the table to unlock business potential and to support the leader in his or her endeavours.
- Is not afraid to 'tell things as they are'.

I have included a case study of one of our current clients to bring to life the value of a working mentor/coach relationship. The name is changed for obvious reasons.

Case Study

(NAME CHANGED)

Jonathan was the managing director of a leading manufacturer that led a global market. Following early successes, it was clear that the business was plateauing. After a number of challenging customer situations, a failed audit and people issues, Jonathan began to lose confidence in his ability to continue the excellent growth of the business.

Jonathan turned to [W]sq solutions to help unlock his and the business's potential. A mentoring and coaching approach was applicable to Jonathan because:

- the mentoring session allowed Jonathan to discuss sensitive issues confidentially without the judgement that could come from those within the organisation
- the coaching session helped provide Jonathan with the tools to analyse the business critically and to come up with a clear strategy to move the business forward.

Within a few sessions Jonathan regained his confidence, the issues with key personnel were addressed and he was able to set some clear targets for the business to move forward. Using delegation tools allowed Jonathan to delegate but not lose control. Our listening ear allowed Jonathan to feel that he could share his frustrations about the business, knowing that he would come away with solutions to move things forward.

The business continues to grow, up 35% on revenue to nearly £18m and 50% on profitability, with the next phase of the five-year growth plan underway to strengthen the executive team in preparation for the business to exit.

9

Thou shalt not despise the importance of rest and health on you and your staff!

What do rest and health have to do with business growth? Check out the statistics.

- In the Netherlands, more than one in eight employees had burn-out complaints in 2011. These complaints are relatively common among employees who work under pressure and employees who have little social support from colleagues and management.[xiii]
- In Fort Worth, Texas, business failure statistics provide grim reading; an evaluation identified that more than 85% of businesses fail before they hit the five-year mark.[xiv]
- The typical business executive in the UK works on average more than sixty hours a week.[xv]
- When looking at executive burnout or derailment, the numbers should cause any board member, executive, CEO or other interested party to pause. More than 60% of individuals in what are considered executive positions reported feeling high stress and anxiety on a regular basis. More than 75% of executives in non-profit organizations claimed that they could not see themselves in the same job in five years.[xvi]
- The impact is seen in the number of sick days taken for psychological/stress-related illnesses and in health care costs. The average executive's health costs are 50% higher than middle management.
- In Japan, more than 2000 Japanese killed themselves due to work-related stress in 2016. Some employees logged more than eighty hours of overtime each month[xvii].

Tony DeHart, although physically healthy, understood first hand the fall out of a hectic, business-driven lifestyle. He talked to Anne Fisher of Fortune Small Business magazine about three mistakes that cost him his marriage. These are his comments on the third mistake:

And the third mistake? Ah, friends, this one's the real biggie. "I underestimated how much time the business was going to take away from my family," he says. "I was literally never home. Our marriage almost didn't survive. I got to the point where I had to say to her, 'I'll do anything. Just please don't leave.' "The wake-up call came when the DeHarts discovered they were going to have a second child, who is now 5 months old. "We had been growing apart for a long time, but that was when we really had to sit down and say, 'Okay, what are we doing here? Where are we headed?'"[xviii]

Our experience has shown that, as a business grows, there must be a proportionate amount of rest and down time to handle the increasing pressure. However, I empathise with many executives who find themselves between a rock and a hard place, especially those who have not created a solid team around them to share the load.

If you wish to be at the helm of a growing business, you must be in the best possible shape. As the business grows, it will become more complex and the decisions that you need to make become larger, more important and more frequent.

I learned this lesson in October 2012. After taking a business leaders' breakfast session with a small group of CEO/MDs, I realised that my leg was swelling rapidly and I was suffering shortness of breath. The next morning, my doctor told me that she believed I had Deep Vein Thrombosis (DVT). A few days later, an ultrasound test confirmed this.

From my perspective at the time, there was no real reason for this. I had not been flying and was not doing anything to trigger it. But during the six week period of recuperation, it was clear to me that two things could have contributed to this condition over a period of time.

- Dehydration; I am not a big tea or coffee drinker and my water intake was very poor.
- My exercise regime was sporadic, bordering on non-existent. My business lifestyle was such that I did not set aside definite, regular times to go to the gym or exercise. In addition, I drove to meetings, sat through them, then sat at my desk back in the office in front of the computer. I sat through most of the day! In more than 10 years of running the business, my lack of activity had also contributed to me gaining at least 25lb in weight!

For me, the DVT was a wakeup call; its diagnosis was 'a bullet dodged'. If I wanted to realise the vision for the investments I'd made in a number of my business propositions, then I had to change my lifestyle and get fit.

Rest is another underestimated need; your body needs sleep to regenerate its cells, including those in the brain. One example from my life will help to make this point clear.

I was asked by the CEO of a group headed by a famous venture capitalist (VC) to turn around a failing organisation. My arrival was the last throw of the dice for the VC to save what was believed to be a business that was not achieving its potential.

In the first few weeks, I travelled the 110 miles to the company daily, leaving at 6:30 in the morning and returning home between 7:30 to 8pm. Although the distance was not too far, the journey was complex as it involved driving on the M20 and M25 motorways. Those of you who know the M25 will be familiar with the words 'roadworks' and 'accidents'. The journey made me late to work or home on many occasions. However, the real impact was in reducing my ability to think on my feet during the day. The truth was that I was overtired and not getting enough rest.

Once I realised this, I found a room to rent from Monday to Thursday and went home on Friday to spend the weekend with my family. The benefits were immediate; I could get back to my lodgings in good time and unwind, play sport and regularly attend the gym. I missed my family during that short season, but software such as Skype was a great way for keeping in touch with them.

You'll be pleased to know that the business was saved, its revenue doubled and, more importantly, for the first time it made a profit for that year!

This next section may make for uncomfortable reading. However, it is necessary; you need to put in place contingency plans. Not having these will hinder the growth of the business, or even kill it overnight. Consider the following points.

- If you die, who will take over the company? Key-man insurance could help to provide funds for your spouse or a key business person that you trust to keep the company going, or to hire someone to run the business or wind it down in an orderly fashion.
- Do you want your spouse or next of kin to be the major shareholder in the business if you die suddenly? There are ways to structure shareholders agreements to ensure that the company buys out your shares at market value to provide a lump sum for your spouse.
- Make sure you have a signed will that encompasses your wishes for your business. Have appropriate health insurance and life insurance in place.

So, what are the solutions to ensure that you stay healthy and rested during your business growth journey? Here are my suggestions.

- Have at least one day of rest in a week where you down tools, switch off the business mobile phone and spend time with your family and friends. If God rested one day in a week, then why not you?
- Ensure you take breaks from your desk during the day, even if it is to go for a walk around the company seeing how people are. Go out to lunch rather than eat sandwiches at the desk.
- Be continually hydrated – drink lots of water not coffee. Water helps us to keep our brain active and think clearly.
- Diarise your holidays and breaks. Entrepreneurs invariably don't take all their allotted holidays, but it is important to take as much as you can. Book something with your spouse or partner and ensure it is diarised and your team are aware of it.
- Find a hobby or activity that you enjoy. Doing something else helps the brain to readjust and rewire its thinking. It encourages creativity. Archimedes did not have his Eureka! moment in a university or laboratory but in the bath! Relaxation promotes creativity by letting you see things in a different context.

Wayne Cordeiro, in his excellent presentation, talks about the balance between work, rest and play.[xix] He emphasises the need to 'fill your tank', in other words to always build into your lifestyle activities that you enjoy and that excite you.

What about your staff? It is no good having a chilled-out CEO or MD and the rest of the staff are run ragged. So how can one create a culture which allows the business to grow and to thrive?

Gretchen Spreitzer and Christine Porath at the University of Michigan's Ross School of Business carried out research on a number of organisations across multiple sectors. They identified that those individuals who thrive in their jobs, through a combination of goal setting and achievement within a learning environment, outperformed those who did not have these elements as part of their working environment.

Gretchen goes on to say:

We think of a thriving workforce as one in which employees are not just satisfied and productive but also engaged in creating the future—the company's and their own. Thriving employees have a bit of an edge—they are highly energized—but they know how to avoid burnout.

Across industries and job types, we found that people who fit our description of thriving demonstrated 16% better overall performance (as reported by their managers) and 125% less burnout (self-reported) than their peers. They were 32% more committed to the organization and 46% more satisfied with their jobs. They also missed much less work and reported significantly fewer doctor visits, which meant health care savings and less lost time for the company.

We've identified two components of thriving. The combination of vitality and learning leads to employees who deliver results and find ways to grow. Their work is rewarding not just because they successfully perform what's expected of them today but also because they have a sense of where they and the company are headed. In short, they are thriving, and the energy they create is contagious.

The two components work in concert; one without the other is unlikely to be sustainable and may even damage performance.[xx]

As we mentioned in Chapter 1, matching an individual's performance to the vision of the business and providing them with ongoing training to achieve their goals, provides an environment that minimises workplace stress as well as providing a focus for driving performance and growth.

To reiterate, it is always worth encouraging your team to get a good work / life balance. Insist that they take their holidays and do not work seven days a week. As a leader, you can model the right behaviour. If you are constantly emailing them about activities on a Sunday evening, it is likely they will fall into the same habits. The team around you must be in tip-top condition to help you grow your business. Look after them and the business will fly.

10

Thou shalt master the art of Leadership.

Is leadership innate or learnt? This question is probably the most frequently asked when I give speeches and presentations about this subject. I believe it a combination of the two.

There are individuals who have an inherent ability to lead people and teams; they have the appropriate skills to motivate others by doing things, or speaking, in a way that endears them to those they lead. Others have to work out these principles; they may have great vision but have problems in articulating their thoughts in a structured way, or they may not have the ability to communicate coherently but discuss things at inappropriate times or miss body-language signals, etc.

In both these instances, the leader may have mastered many of the disciplines of leadership but still fall short in one or more areas. What is important is to recognise potential and develop the skills and the art of leadership.

The art of leadership

Leadership is an art form. Great leaders litter the history of the world and they are always known for the thing that they did best. There are countless excellent books about leadership; I think Allan Leighton's is probably the best.[xxi]

My aim here is to outline some key principles to help you develop your learning and understanding of leadership. These are the five qualities that I believe make a great leader.

They know their strengths

Great leaders understand their strengths and maximise them. René Carayol describes this succinctly when he says that the best leaders are Olympian in two or three areas.[xxii]

A good example of a leader who knows his strengths is Richard Branson. He has a great eye for identifying business opportunities in underperforming markets and he understands how to build a brand through PR, culture and reputation. He epitomises the Virgin Brand; whenever a new Virgin organisation is created, he provides the initial 'frontman' launch to give the new company validation and momentum. However, he always employs great leaders to run these organisations, giving him the freedom to do what he does best – identify the next big thing!

Although good business leaders believe in themselves and their skills, they often forget that it is essential to bring in new talent as the business grows in order to introduce new systems and processes to propel the business to the next level. These experienced individuals may need to be paid a good rate (even higher than you are currently paid). Taking the short-term view will only stifle the dream that you wish to achieve.

They get a great team around them

Good leaders always seek out talent. They understand that they need not only the mavericks but also detail-oriented individuals in the team. Many leaders make the mistake of choosing individuals just like themselves, but a business demands personalities that can meet its demands. An introvert may be terrible in a sales situation but ideal for preparing due-diligence papers for an acquisition or an important negotiation with a supplier. It is imperative therefore, that leaders understand their strengths and weaknesses so they can rally the right individuals around them to support them in areas where they are less comfortable.

Sir Terry Leahy, the former CEO of Tesco's, is passionate about identifying talent and getting a team around him. Having risen through the ranks, he believes that there are chief executives buried under a pile of printouts in a back office somewhere. In the organisation, there was a process to identify the top 10% who could be moved to the next level of management. This focus is essential if one is looking for the brightest and the most able leaders of tomorrow. Succession planning is easier when there is already a culture of identifying talent in the organisation.

They are masters of delegation but do not lose control

Many leaders have problems with delegation because they believe that they are the only ones that can carry out the required tasks. However, the key principle in delegation is to ensure that there are appropriate systems and processes in place to allow you to keep track of the key performance indicators. This means your grasp of the key numbers in the business must be in place before you delegate a task or activity.

Once the numbers are grasped and the activity delegated, then a regular review mechanism must be put in place to enable accountability. Vernon Harnish's *Mastering the Rockefeller Habits* outlines the importance of weekly, monthly and quarterly meetings which are action-driven and focus on the key performances of the business, identifying trends and recommending appropriate actions and solutions.[xxiii]

Sir Philip Green is known as the master of delegation. Although he runs a multi-billion operation, he still manages to answer 98% of his calls in twenty-four hours and makes major decisions within three minutes, with a yes/no response. His ability to use numbers to make informed decisions allows him to 'cut to the chase'. However, from being a respected business leader, Sir Philip Green is now spoken of in pejorative terms. Reports about his leadership style and ethics have tarnished the star of this once respected leader.[xxiv] A lesson for us all!

Leaders understand the importance of satisfying and delighting customers

This passion is one of the essential qualities of great leaders. The customer is seen as king, therefore the leader ensures that *all* processes in the organisation are centred on maintaining that focus.

In order to have this focus, there must be a culture of 'yes, we can' rather than 'the computer says no'. Innovation and creating new ways to solve the customer's 'pain' are key aspects of forging strong relationships with clients. Going the extra mile is also important in retaining and delighting them.

An example from my own career was when leading a software company that had developed a market-leading track-and-trace solution for the healthcare market. At the time, I was staying away from my young family during the week and looked forward to catching up with them at the weekend. One week, we had planned to go away on Saturday to do some fun stuff. While getting ready to go, I received a call from my sales director. 'Wayne,' he said, 'we have a major problem.'

A key customer's production site was due to go live on the Monday and our software, which runs the site, was not working. This was a £1m contract, and the potential consequences were not worth thinking about. In my head, all I wanted to do was spend time with my family, but reason prevailed and

I got ready to leave. Although I had an operations director overseeing the implementation, it was important for me to impress on the customer that we were taking the issue seriously by having the managing director (me) on site.

I called the senior software developer and the IT director and ordered a team to join me in Leeds that Saturday afternoon. We had seven people over three days staying in hotels and working on site to ensure that the software performed. This situation not only saved the business but led to a strong relationship with the client, one that is still active today.

Leaders achieve extraordinary performance from their people

My final thought is possibly the most obvious but often the least acted on and understood in the companies that we have helped to grow. The power a leader has to motivate staff, as well as set the culture of the business to achieve above average performance, is evident throughout our history. Everyone is capable of extraordinary performance and the best leaders can extract this from their people. Lord Browne, the former BP boss, encourages leaders to 'protect, cajole and inspire everyone around you, align them to what you are doing'.

You may ask 'How do I motivate my people?'. Good question. Here are a few suggestions.

- Articulate the vision of where you want to go. People want to be led; they are passionate about causes with a clear destination. Paint the destination in simple terms so that people can understand. More importantly, help them to appreciate that what they do, however little, is essential to fulfil the vision.
- Model the culture and values that you want in the business. A strong company culture tells your staff, customers and suppliers the key elements of how business is to be conducted and executed. Good culture frames and protects the business brand and minimises future risks. Tesco's fine for overstating profits could have been prevented through a strong ethical culture modelled within the board.[xxv]

- Be visible and 'walk the talk'. Know your people wherever possible; take interest in the little things they do and say. If necessary, spend a day in their shoes. You will be surprised at what you find.
- Reward wherever possible. This does not have to be monetary – it could be dinner for two, sports tickets, a fun family day, etc. Allan Leighton, in his *On Leadership*, quotes a lovely example of Julian Richer of Richer Sounds lending the company Rolls Royce to the best-performing branch every month. You may not have a Rolls Royce, but the point is to make a creative activity that allows people to remember the purpose of their role and that their work matters.
- Saying thank you and well done. You may be asking yourself, 'Why should I say thank you for doing the job I pay them to do?' From our perspective, gratitude shows each individual that he or she is valued and appreciated.

We could go on and define a host of characteristics of great leaders but it is important to note that companies that have exhibited extraordinary performance can largely attribute it to a clear vision, strong culture and exceptional leadership performance. These are vital in moving your business to the next level.

References

i The Bible; Proverbs 29:18

ii www.toms.com

iii www.salesforce.com

iv www.dictionary.com

v dailymail.co.uk/news/article-7464871/Top-British-firms-hit-Google-Facebook-stifling-competition-online.html

vi How the Mighty Fall: And Why some companies never give in (ISBN: 9780977326419)

vii http://www.franklin-electric.com/corporate/investors/financial/pr_files/2010/Franklin_Electric_3rd_Quarter_2010_Earnings_Release.pdf

viii Good Finance Guide for Small Businesses: How to Raise, Manage and Grow your Company's Cash (Business), (ISBN-13: 9780713682090)

ix http://www.gallup.com/poll/1654/honesty-ethics-professions.aspx

x https://www.theguardian.com/sustainable-business/ethical-business-trust-values

xi http://www.theglobeandmail.com/report-on-business/industry-news/energy-and-resources/bp-sues-halliburton-over-42-billion-oil-spill-bill/article2289618/

xii http://www.adweek.com/adfreak/chapstick-gets-itself-social-media-death-spiral-136097

xiii https://www.ncbi.nlm.nih.gov/pmc/articles/PMC5974116/

xiv https://northdallasirshelp.com/the-most-likely-reasons-why-small-businesses-fail-in-north-dallas-area/

xv https://www.cnbc.com/2018/06/20/harvard-study-what-ceos-do-all-day.html